955
HAS

C·1

3 4880 05000724 9
Haskins, James.

Count your way
through Iran

$16.94

DATE DUE	BORROWER'S NAME	ROOM NO.

955
HAS

C·1

3 4880 05000724 9
Haskins, James.

Count your way
through Iran

Count Your Way through
Iran

by **Jim Haskins** and **Kathleen Benson**

illustrations by **Farida Zaman**

Ⓜ Millbrook Press / Minneapolis

To Markeise Tucker, Jemyron Gillon, Aaron Gillon, Rashad Gillon, and Chaundra Gillon –K. B.

For Riz, who loves to travel –F. Z.

Text copyright © 2007 by Jim Haskins and Kathleen Benson
Illustrations copyright © 2007 by Millbrook Press, Inc.

Millbrook Press, Inc.
A division of Lerner Publishing Group
241 First Avenue North
Minneapolis, Minnesota 55401 U.S.A.

Website address: www.lernerbooks.com

Library of Congress Cataloging-in-Publication Data

Haskins, James, 1941–
    Count your way through Iran / by Jim Haskins and Kathleen
  Benson ; illustrations by Farida Zaman.
      p. cm. — (Count your way)
    ISBN-13: 978–1–57505–881–8 (lib. bdg. : alk. paper)
    ISBN-10: 1–57505–881–2 (lib. bdg. : alk. paper)
    1. Iran—Civilization—Juvenile literature. 2. Persian
  language—Numerals—Juvenile literature. 3. Counting—
  Juvenile literature. I. Benson, Kathleen. II. Zaman, Farida, 1963-
  III. Title. IV. Series: Haskins, James, 1941- Count your way.
  DS254.75.H37 2007
  955—dc   222005033159

Manufactured in the United States of America
1 2 3 4 5 6 – DP – 12 11 10 09 08 07

Introduction

The country of Iran is in the Middle East. Its official name is the Islamic Republic of Iran. It has an area of 636,296 square miles. Iran is almost as large as Alaska. Nearly 70 million people live in the country. Iran used to be called Persia. The country's official language is Persian. Persian can also be called Farsi. Farsi is written with the Arabic alphabet. This alphabet is read from right to left.

1 ١ (yek)

Iran makes **one** national car. It is called the *Paykan*. Paykan is the Farsi word for "arrow." The car is made only in Iran. Iran has a lot of oil. Some of the oil is made into gasoline for cars. But not all Iranians have cars. People who cannot afford a car take taxis or ride buses.

2 ٢ (doh)

The **two** Towers of Silence stand on two hills in the desert.
They are in the middle of Iran near the city of Yazd. The towers
are from ancient times. People who believed in the Zoroastrian
(zo-ro-AHS-tree-in) religion built them. Only a small number
of people in Iran still follow this religion. Yazd was a center
for Zoroastrians. A temple lies near the Towers of Silence.
The temple holds a special flame that has burned for
more than one thousand years.

3 ٣ (say)

Iran's flag has **three** colors. White is for peace. Red stands for courage. Green is the color of Islam. Islam is the official religion of Iran. The followers of Islam are called Muslims. The red shape in the middle of the flag stands for the word *Allah*. Allah is the Muslim name for *God*. The words *Allahu Akbar* are written at the bottom of the green band and the top of the red band. This means "God is Great."

 **(cha-haar)**

A man writes **four** lines in Persian. He is a poet named Omar Khayyam (OH-mar Kai-YAHM), and he lived nine hundred years ago. His four-line poems made him famous. Many of them are in a book called *The Rubaiyat of Omar Khayyam.* Omar Khayyam also studied math and science. He created a calendar and made maps of the stars.

5 ۵ (panj)

Five women weave a carpet. The wool they use
is dyed many colors. The women weave the
carpet on a large loom. They look at a pattern
that tells them how to create the fancy design.
Some weavers also make their own designs
as they go. Persian rugs are known
around the world for their beauty.

6 ۶ (shesh)

The tar has **six** strings. *Tar* means "string" in Farsi. The tar is a little like a guitar. Its body is made from mulberry wood. Lambskin is stretched behind the strings. Musicians use the tar to play traditional Iranian tunes. Some tar players sing songs while they play. Many of the songs are religious.

 **7** ٧ **(haft)**

Iran borders on **seven** countries. They are Iraq, Turkey, Armenia, Azerbaijan, Turkmenistan, Afghanistan, and Pakistan. The Caspian Sea is to the north, between Azerbaijan and Turkmenistan. The Persian Gulf and the Gulf of Oman are to the south. A gulf is a section of the ocean that is partly surrounded by land.

8  (hasht)

Eight animals found in the Caspian Sea are sturgeon, herring, perch, carp, catfish, Dalmatian pelicans, Caspian seals, and Caspian pond turtles. The Caspian Sea is the largest lake in the world. It is almost as big as Montana. The water in the Caspian Sea is salt water. People cannot drink salt water. But Iranians catch many fish from the Caspian Sea.

Perch

9 9 (noh)

Nine pistachio trees grow in the groves of southern Iran. A pistachio tree can produce nuts for more than one hundred years. Pistachios are one of Iran's main exports. An export is something a country sells to another country. Iranians add these nuts to main dishes and desserts. Roasted pistachios also make a tasty snack.

10 ١٠ (dah)

Ten wrestlers train together. They are in a gym called a *zurkhaneh* (zur-hah-NAY). This word means "house of power." The wrestlers perform dances and movements to show their strength. A leader directs the athletes by chanting poems and playing a drum. Wrestling is one of the most popular sports in Iran.

Pronunciation Guide

1 / ١ / yek

2 / ٢ / doh

3 / ٣ / say

4 / ۴ / cha-haar

5 / ۵ / panj

6 / ۶ / shesh

7 / ٧ / haft

8 / ٨ / hasht

9 / ٩ / noh

10 / ١٠ / dah